Living It Up in Space

PATHFINDER EDITION

By Nancy Finton

CONTENTS

LIVING IT UP IN SPAC

What's it like to live 220 miles above Earth, flying faster than a speeding bullet through dark, airless space? We asked a space station commander!

BY NANCY FINTON

As you read these words, people are whizzing around Earth at 17,000 miles per hour. They are traveling in a giant, **orbiting** laboratory. It's called the International Space Station, or ISS.

The ISS is a huge team effort. The United States, Russia, Japan, Canada, Brazil, and 11 European countries that make up the European Space Agency are building the station. When completed, it will be larger than a football field and weigh up to a million pounds. Nothing that big and heavy could be rocketed into space.

That's why scientists couldn't put the ISS together on Earth. Instead, they launched pieces of the station into space, one or two at a time. The pieces traveled into space on shuttles and rockets. The first pieces were sent in 1998. When they got there, astronauts began putting the station together. They were working 220 miles above Earth! The first astronauts to live aboard the station arrived in 2000.

Inside the ISS, astronauts find protection against deadly space conditions, such as lack of air and temperatures that bounce from minus 250°F to 250°F. Still, life on a space station can get a little weird. Imagine living without the **gravity** that keeps you on your chair and your pencil on your desk. People on orbiting spacecraft float in **microgravity**. This is a condition in which the effects of gravity are greatly reduced. It's sometimes described as "weightlessness."

Getting Around
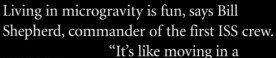

Living in microgravity is fun, says Bill Shepherd, commander of the first ISS crew. "It's like moving in a swimming pool, only you're even lighter. You can push off with a fingertip and move across the whole space **module**," he explains. "You can look at any place on the wall or ceiling and go there."

Shepherd spent months on the ISS during his first mission. "After coming back to Earth," he says, "it took me a week to get used to walking around again."

Dressed for Success.
Bill Shepherd didn't need a space suit inside the ISS. But no astronaut can work outside the station without one.
NASA

CE

Light Snack.
Tuna can act a little fishy in microgravity. This astronaut's tuna is floating up and out of its can!

Daily Workout.
Running on a treadmill in space requires a harness. Otherwise, the astronaut would just be running in air.

NASA

Wall-to-Wall Sleeping

In microgravity there's no need for a bed. Astronauts can snooze while floating upside down in the middle of a room. But there's a chance they could "drift off" and bump against computer controls. So at night, they strap themselves into sleeping bags that hang from the walls.

"Sleeping in space is very relaxing," Shepherd says. "You're not weighed down by gravity, so you don't feel anything pressing on your skin."

Bathroom Activities

In microgravity, water from a shower flies in all directions. Floating water droplets could damage ISS computers. So instead of taking showers, space station residents rub water and soap over their bodies, then sponge off.

In orbit, you can't rely on gravity to tug wastewater down the pipes of a toilet. The space model works like a vacuum cleaner, using a stream of air to pull waste into sealed containers. The containers are then sent off in spacecraft that land on Earth, or in smaller craft designed to burn up in Earth's **atmosphere**.

No More Mushed Chicken

Supply ships bring meals to the station only once in a while. That means astronaut food needs to stay fresh a long time.

Foods like chicken and peas used to be kept fresh by mushing them up and sealing them in tubes. At mealtime, astronauts would squirt out the food like toothpaste.

Luckily, scientists found new ways to kill the **microbes** that make food rot. Some space foods, such as scrambled eggs and fruit punch, are dried out. Astronauts just add water. Presto! The food is ready to eat.

Other foods, such as hot dogs and beef stew, are sealed in microbe-blocking plastic bags. Astronauts heat the bags before mealtime. Treats like candy and gum can stay fresh for a month without help.

"I thought the Russian food was a little tastier than the American food," Shepherd says. "They had good soups—chicken and rice was my favorite. But no one was very picky."

To keep their meals from floating away, astronauts often slot food packages into special trays, then strap the trays to their legs.

Work and Play

ISS astronauts keep busy. You're most likely to find them doing science experiments, walking in space to connect a new module, or working out on special gym equipment. (Astronauts must do a lot of exercising. Muscles go soft quickly when they don't have to work against strong gravity.)

As the first crew, Shepherd's team had a special task: testing and repairing all the station's equipment. "We worked from 6:30 in the morning until 9:30 at night," he says.

When he could snatch a free moment, Shepherd liked to e-mail folks back home, snap pictures of Earth, read books, and watch movies. "Once we had a *Lethal Weapon* week. We watched all four of them!" he says.

What's the Point?

It will cost the United States billions of dollars to build its part of the ISS. Other countries are spending billions of dollars too. Why are people willing to pay so much for a station in space? Without Earth's atmosphere in the way, ISS astronauts can take clear pictures of outer space. And they can snap distance shots of Earth that will help scientists track changes in pollution, rain forest destruction, and climate.

Astronauts will also conduct experiments to learn how materials and living things react to long periods in microgravity. This could help scientists create lifesaving drugs and stronger building materials to use on Earth.

"This could be the start of an era where people don't just live on the Earth anymore," Shepherd says. "I think we could fly a mission that looked very much like the one we were just on that would get humans to Mars. I would be very interested in being a part of that mission."

NASA

Ups and Downs.
Two former crew members pose inside the U.S. laboratory module called Destiny. The ISS labs will let scientists conduct experiments too delicate to do in Earth's gravity.

INTERNATIONAL SPACE STATION

When it is completed, the International Space Station (ISS) will be the largest human-made object in space. Here's how it will look.

Crew return vehicle
(out of view)

Truss

European Space Agency research module

Japanese research module Kibo (Hope)

Solar-array panel

Building the Station, Piece by Piece

Building the ISS will require more than 40 trips into space and 1,500 hours of spacewalking.

Crew Return Vehicle
Astronauts need a quick way to return to Earth—just in case. NASA is designing a seven-person vehicle. A smaller Russian Soyuz craft is now on hand for the current crew.

Trusses
These are beams that support other ISS pieces.

Research Modules
Here scientists will see how chemicals, plants, and animals behave in long periods of microgravity.

Solar-Array Panels
The ISS needs a lot of electrical power. The sun's rays are very strong in space. Giant solar panels take in these strong rays and turn their energy into electricity.

Russian Service Module (Zvezda)
This section holds all the computers that control the space station. It also provides a living space for three astronauts.

Russian service module Zvezda (Star)

Russian control module Zarya (Sunrise)

Radiator

Mechanical Arm

Habitation Module

Habitation module

Exercise and medical stations

Sleep and work stations

Eating and meeting areas

Russian Control Module (Zarya)
This module stores fuel and provides power during early stages of ISS assembly.

Radiators
Machines that control the ISS give off lots of heat. Too much heat could start a fire. Radiators carry this heat away from the station and release it into space.

Mechanical Arms
These giant robotic arms grab modules or big equipment and move them into place, holding them while astronauts assemble the station.

Habitation Module
This would be home for at least six astronauts. It would include sleep stations, a kitchen area, a toilet, and a washing area.

Suited **for** **Spacewalking**

pace is definitely not user-friendly. Astronauts would die within minutes if they stepped outside the International Space Station without their space suits. Wearing the high-tech suits, they can walk in space for hours to work on the station.

Headlights on helmet

Backpack

Pocket lined with bristles

Adult-size diapers

Tethers

Fourteen layers of material

Outer layers made of Kevlar and Teflon

NASA

Your Mission

Read the list of "unfriendly conditions" that astronauts encounter in space. Match each condition to one "space suit solution."

When you're finished, look at the letters in your answers. If they're correct, they will spell out a space word! (One letter is used twice.)

Unfriendly Conditions

1. There is no air in space for astronauts to breathe.

2. Small rocks shoot through space at thousands of miles per hour. At that speed, even a speck of dust could harm a spacewalker.

3. Space temperatures soar to 250°F in the sun and plunge to minus 250°F in the shade.

4. There are no high-tech toilets to use during long spacewalks.

5. During half of all spacewalks, astronauts work in the dark.

6. In orbit, littering can be deadly. Tossed trash will travel fast enough to harm a spaceship.

7. Gravity doesn't hold things down in space. If an astronaut started to float away, he or she might drift in that direction forever.

Space Suit Solutions

 E Spacewalkers tie themselves to a spacecraft with at least two safety lines.

 H The outer layers of a space suit are made of supertough materials like Kevlar and Teflon.

 L A space suit has a pocket with wire bristles that keeps objects from dropping into space.

 T Spacewalkers wear adult-size diapers under their suits.

 U Fourteen layers of material keep heat from moving into or out of the suit.

S A backpack with a tank feeds air into the space suit.

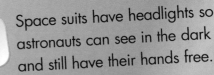 **T** Space suits have headlights so astronauts can see in the dark and still have their hands free.

9

Out of

Astronauts face many challenges—from the ordinary to the extraordinary. Here are some questions and answers about what it's like to live in space.

This World!

How are astronauts chosen?

Every two years, NASA selects new astronauts. Thousands of people apply. Only about 100 are chosen.

Most people decided early in life that they wanted to be an astronaut. They worked hard in school. They did well in math and science.

Astronauts also need to function well as part of a team. During their time in space, they share everything. They live in close quarters with many other people. There's no room for arguments on a spacecraft!

So the answer is: Anyone can become an astronaut. But you need the right training, skills, and personality.

How do astronauts get water?

Think of all the water people use in a day. We need it for cooking, cleaning, washing dishes, taking showers, flushing toilets, and brushing teeth. That's a lot of water.

Like air, water is essential for life. In space, it's also hard to get. In fact, water has to be delivered from Earth. So astronauts can't afford to waste a single drop. Once water is used on the ISS, it gets collected. Then it's cleaned and the water is used again.

In fact, astronauts recycle almost all the water they have. They use the water from sinks and other systems on the spacecraft. They even collect the sweat inside space suits!

What if an astronaut feels sick?

Many astronauts get sick during their first few days in space. That's because their bodies aren't used to living in microgravity.

Imagine not knowing which way is up. You start feeling confused and queasy. This feeling is called "space sickness."

Space sickness happens when you're not used to the way your body is moving. For example, an astronaut might feel sick when she is floating inside the spacecraft. That's because she is used to gravity pulling her feet to the ground. So the feeling of drifting around in space makes her ill.

Astronauts quickly get over their space sickness. After about three days, the sickness goes away. The astronauts' bodies get used to the feeling of living in space.

What happens if there is a fire?

Fires might be an astronaut's biggest worry. If your home catches fire, you get out as fast as you can. In space, however, you can't escape. You don't have anywhere else to go!

Fires also burn a bit differently in space. On Earth, the flames blaze upward. It's a different story inside a spacecraft.

That's because air is sent into the ship through vents in the walls and ceilings. Instead of burning upward, the flames blaze toward the vents. That means the fire could travel in many directions at once.

So spacecraft are made of materials that don't burn easily. They also have many tools to put out fires. And of course, spacecraft have warning systems to let astronauts know if a fire has begun.

Life in Space

It's time to suit up and discover what you learned about living in space.

1 How is the International Space Station a team effort?

2 What is microgravity? How does it affect astronauts?

3 How does sleeping in space compare to sleeping on Earth?

4 What training and skills do astronauts have?

5 Why is living in space dangerous?